THE TREE OF CHASTITY

Borgo Press Books by JEAN-FRANÇOIS REGNARD

The Tree of Chastity and Other Plays (with Charles Dufresny)

Borgo Press Books by CHARLES DUFRESNY

The Spirit of Contradiction & The Double Wedding
Straight from the Convent & The Interrupted Wedding (with Florent Dancourt)
The Tree of Chastity and Other Plays (with Jean-François Regnard)
The Village Coquette & The Crazy Wager (with Florent Dancourt)

THE TREE OF CHASTITY

AND OTHER PLAYS

JEAN-FRANÇOIS

REGNARD

With Charles Dufresny
Translated and Adapted by Frank J. Morlock

THE BORGO PRESS
MMXIII

THE TREE OF CHASTITY

Copyright © 1986, 2002, 2013 by Frank J. Morlock

FIRST EDITION

Published by Wildside Press LLC

www.wildsidebooks.com

DEDICATION

For My Dear Friend, Tony Smith

CONTENTS

THE TREE OF CHASTITY, with Charles
   Dufresny. 9
   CAST OF CHARACTERS. 10
   THE PLAY. 11
WAIT FOR ME UNDER THE ELM 59
   CAST OF CHARACTERS. 60
   THE PLAY. 61
THE UNFORESEEN RETURN. 113
   CAST OF CHARACTERS. 114
   THE PLAY. 115
**THE RIDICULOUS MERCHANT: A COMIC
   OPERA**. 175
   CAST OF CHARACTERS. 176
   THE PLAY. 177
ABOUT THE TRANSLATOR. 189

THE TREE OF CHASTITY
WITH CHARLES DUFRESNY

CAST OF CHARACTERS

Peasant, father of Jaqueline

Jaqueline, his daughter

Pierrot, in love with Jaqueline

Columbine, in love with Pierrot

Harlequin, guardian of the Tree

Octavio, a shepherd

Scaramouche, an old man

Mezzetin, his son

Catos, a cousin of Harlequin's

Old Lady

Six men, four women

THE PLAY

The scene represents a square before a large Tree. The Tree is hollow, and the hollow is large enough for a person to step inside. There is a bow hung over the opening. There are some tents around the Tree and several tombs. A sign says: The Tree of Lucretia. Harlequin sits at a booth which has a sign saying: Guardian of the Sacred Tree of Chastity.

Harlequin

There are lots of things to consider when you think about marrying a country girl. If you ask her: "Would you like to take a walk?" she replies: "To be sure, sir." "Would you like me to kiss—your hand?" "To be sure, sir." "Would you like me to—?" "To be sure, sir." Agreeable always—to be sure! But what's this girl coming here want? She must be a Parisienne, because she intends to turn a man's head. Never did a nymph of the Tuileries do the tricks better by moonlight. Better let her make all the advances—that's the fashion these days.

(Columbine enters and curtsies to Harlequin.)

Harlequin (ignoring her)

La, la, la—

(Columbine curtsies again.)

(whistling)

Whee—

Columbine (furiously to herself)

So! One only gets scorn for throwing oneself at a man's head. I shall be proud. (turning away in a huff)

Harlequin

The girl must be stupid to be so easily discouraged. Well, I am not simpleton enough to let her go. (to Columbine) Madame—can one ask—what time is it? Don't you have a watch?

Columbine

My watch isn't working.

Harlequin

Women have charming little watches which sometimes mark the time for love.

Columbine

This watch doesn't ring for you.

Harlequin

Had I the good fortune to—see in the shadow of the dial of the sun of your beautiful eyes—

Columbine

I am only the dial of the frigid moon. (lifting her veil) Stop the nonsense. We've known each other a long time.

Harlequin

Decidedly, I've seen that face before. Didn't we study together?

Columbine

Yes. We were in service at Paris.

Harlequin

Peace, peace, let's not talk of being in service. I have risen in this village to be a man of consequence.

Columbine

So I heard. You are guardian of the Tree of Lucretia.

And that's why I wish to renew my acquaintance with you. So that you can help me.

Harlequin

If you wish to prove your chastity—

Columbine

Certainly not.

Harlequin

You relieve my mind.

Columbine

Enough of your stupid jokes. Will you help me?

Harlequin

Willingly, provided you say nothing of our old acquaintance.

Columbine

Do you know a certain Pierrot?

Harlequin

To my cost. This Pierrot has taken all my hopes from me. He is going to marry my beautiful Jaqueline. Boo hoo.

Columbine

Then indeed, we have common interest. I wish to marry Pierrot. You wish to marry Jaqueline. We must work in concert to prevent their marriage.

Harlequin

I dream of it every minute.

Columbine

Pierrot loves me.

Harlequin

And I, I love Jaqueline.

Columbine

Listen to the way I've devised to prevent the marriage. Pierrot wants Jacqueline to prove her chastity before they marry. To do this he will ask her to sit in the Tree of Lucretia. Now if— But here is Pierrot with Jaqueline's father.

Harlequin

I had better prepare for the Ceremony of the Tree.

(Exit Harlequin. Enter Pierrot and the Peasant.)

Pierrot

I tell you, I am as obstinate as an old doctor.

Peasant

But you're not reasonable. Hold on, here's Columbine who will decide for us.

Pierrot

I don't like it, no, I don't like it at all. I once offered to marry her, and a girl always bears a grudge against those who start something and don't finish it.

Columbine (aside to Pierrot)

No, no, I will take your side—don't worry.

Pierrot

I ask you to excuse my deserting you to marry Jaqueline. Please don't feel bad. I will marry you some other time.

Columbine

Yes, yes, there will be an opportunity.

Peasant

Columbine—you be the judge. Isn't Pierrot wrong to demand that my daughter prove her purity by coming to the Tree? She's a young girl who's always been under lock and key, carefully guarded.

Columbine

But that proves nothing. Didn't you ever hear of a passkey?

Peasant

My late wife always watched her with the utmost care.

Columbine

Your wife may have had those distractions which make it hard for the guardian to guard herself.

Peasant

My wife was very watchful. A shepherd never guarded his flock better.

Columbine

Yes, but if the watch dog is having a good time rolling around on its back, the wolf soon takes the sheep by the throat.

Peasant

Nonsense. My wife always watched her daughter intently.

Columbine

It wouldn't be the first nesting egg that hatched prematurely. (to Pierrot) There, Pierrot, you see how I take your side?

Peasant (to Pierrot)

If you're so suspicious, why do you want to get married?

Pierrot

Far be it from me to be suspicious. But, when we've got this wonderful Tree that will prove a woman's chastity—I simply don't wish to get married without it. I want Jaqueline to sit in the Tree, and I am going to find Harlequin to prepare the Ceremony.

(Exit Pierrot.)

Columbine

What an obstinate man! But, why do you object to Jaqueline proving her chastity by taking the test? Perhaps, you think her credentials are false?

Peasant

No.

Columbine

Or, do you think the question an insult?

Peasant

No. I understand how Pierrot feels. Very natural. One would like to be sure. But, if she takes the test and passes it, as I'm sure she will, all the other girls in the village will hate her.

Columbine

That's a thought.

Peasant

Why don't you take the test?

Columbine

Me? Why should I do that?

Peasant

You see. No one dares to do it.

Columbine

Oh, I dare. I'd just rather not.

Peasant

Why not?

Columbine

Why not?

Peasant

Why not?

Columbine

Because—

Peasant

That proves my point.

Columbine

Not at all. They say that for the least little thing the Tree will close on a girl and suffocate her. Why risk it?

Peasant

But, it's never happened yet, has it?

Columbine

Not recently, that I know of. But there are moments when a girl is afraid to be honest with herself. And, who can be sure that isn't the case with the Tree? And for that reason, I advise you not to expose your daughter to any such silly test before I've talked to her. Go get her for me, and I will tell you honestly whether she ought to risk this awful test.

Peasant

I am sure of her, but, to please you, I will bring her to talk with you.

(Exit Peasant.)

Columbine

Jaqueline is a big silly—both dumb and stupid. I can't see what either Pierrot or Harlequin can see in her. But I will trap her easily enough. All I have to do is convince her not to sit under the Tree. Pierrot will marry me instead of her, and Harlequin will marry Jaqueline.

(Re-enter Peasant with Jaqueline.)

Peasant

Here, daughter—answer all the questions Miss Columbine asks of you—and don't hide anything from her. It's a question concerning your life.

(Exit Peasant.)

Columbine

Here, my young lady—which do you like most: the villainous Pierrot or the ravishing Harlequin who is always singing at your window?

Jaqueline

I told my father yesterday that it seemed to me that I like Harlequin best. But Dad convinced me that it's Pierrot I want the most and that I must marry him. Father knows best, I guess.

Columbine

Would you like me to teach you how to be wiser than your father in this matter?

Jaqueline

Oh, you would make me very happy.

Columbine

Here's the secret. Imagine that Pierrot is on one side and the adorable Harlequin is on the other. Now, your father says to you: "Jaqueline, one of these two men will be your husband—so kiss him." The one which you go to first is the one you love best—that's certain.

Jaqueline

Oh, truly, then it's Harlequin I love, for I want to kiss him first.

Columbine

Well—if you love Harlequin, it is simple to marry him. Here's how you do it. Pierrot wants you to go to the Tree. Refuse to do it. Pierrot won't want you and Harlequin will marry you.

Jaqueline

To be sure—but everyone will think I'm a bad girl. And, my father says that if that happens to a girl, no one will ever want her. He says it's a fate worse than death—he says—

Columbine

He says, he says— Indeed, I can see you know nothing of the world.

Jaqueline

Oh, lady, I'm a good girl; my father has told me so, and I want to sit under the Tree.

Columbine (aside)

Indeed, I can see I'll have to change my approach. (aloud) Well, then, go under the Tree. Don't wait. Make all your friends hate you. Go, get suffocated.

Jaqueline

The Tree won't suffocate chaste girls.

Columbine

But, are you sure you're chaste?

Jaqueline

Truly, I am. Ask my father.

Columbine

Do you really know what it is to be chaste and pure?

Jaqueline

To be chaste and pure is—is—but, can't one be chaste and pure without knowing what it is?

Columbine

No.

Jaqueline

No?

Columbine

No. I can see your mother had never told you. I am going to explain it to you. It's only a manner of speaking of protecting one's honor.

Jaqueline

Oh!

Columbine

But, there are several ways of losing it.

Jaqueline

Oh! There's more than one way to lose it?

Columbine

Indeed! Have you ever met a wolf?

Jaqueline

Oh, no. I would die of fear.

Columbine (aside)

That won't work. (aloud) Have you ever slept in the

hay, or in a bed of leaves?

Jaqueline

Oh, never. I never go in the woods for fear of mosquitoes.

Columbine (aside)

I'm not getting anywhere. (aloud) Did you ever let the cat get the cheese?

Jaqueline

Hey, does that prevent a girl from being chaste?

Columbine

That'll do it.

Jaqueline

Oh, lady!

Columbine

And, how did this misfortune happen to you?

Jaqueline

One day, I had a little cheese with cream, and the cat came.

Columbine

Horrible! And then?

Jaqueline

I beat the cat, but it wouldn't go away. It became furious—

Columbine

Ah, what misfortune! Well—?

Jaqueline

I dropped the cheese and I ran away.

Columbine

Well, it's certainly time. Aren't you ashamed?

Jaqueline (protesting)

But any girl would have done the same thing in my place. It was a horrible cat. You would've, too.

Columbine

And you are rash enough to expose yourself by coming under the Tree?

Jaqueline

But, Columbine, it was a big cat, and it really wasn't much cheese.

Columbine

Go ahead—the Tree will suffocate you.

Jaqueline

Oh, I won't do it. How miserable I am—

Columbine

You've got to preserve your life—

Jaqueline

But, my reputation—

Columbine

Do you want to die?

Jaqueline

But, Pierrot—

Columbine

He's coming now.

(Enter Pierrot.)

Pierrot (to Jaqueline)

Come on, come on, the bird trap is all ready. I am going to put you right in the middle of that Tree—

Jaqueline

Hey, Pierrot!

Pierrot

What! You tremble already—just seeing the tombstones of sluts that were suffocated by the Tree for their sins?

(Enter Harlequin.)

Harlequin (singing)

Awesome Tree—Roman antiquity.

Planted by chaste Lucretia—

Your sap lives where chastity reigns.

But alas, you are nothing but a rotten stump.

For you died with Lucretia—for lack of company.

The woman of today is but a broken reed—

Who preserves only the leaves of her honor.

O ancient, fatal Tree, your pitiless trunk

Wipes out all unfaithful women.

Ah, if you were planted in the courts of kings

Such places would be barren, and seldom frequented.

(Enter Scaramouche as a sick magistrate followed by Mezzetin, his son.)

Scaramouche (sadly)

Sir—sir—

Harlequin

Has your wife been suffocated by the Tree, sir?

Mezzetin (laughing)

Ah, ah, no, no. My father was never married.

Harlequin

The father cries, the son laughs.

Scaramouche

It's that—it's that—that I am—

Harlequin (mimicking him)

Well—what are you?

Mezzetin (laughing)

Ah, ah, everything my father is telling you is true.

Scaramouche

I am the teacher in our village.

Harlequin

Ah, ah—schoolmaster.

Mezzetin

Ah, ah, it's my father who, ah, it's my father who—ah, he's going to tell you, he's going to tell you—(laughing)

Scaramouche

I am the one who composed—

Mezzetin

Yes, yes, my father did it—ah, ah, all of it. I did some, too—ask him about it, ask him.

Scaramouche

I composed the slanderous songs about the cat who got

the cheese. And the girls who gave it to him. And my son sings them.

Mezzetin

Ah, ah, ah, yes, and we are here to compose songs about the girls who come under the Chastity Tree—ah, ah, because they say today some girl must try it.

Harlequin

And what do you do?

Scaramouche (weeping)

I'm the one who sings the gay songs.

Mezzetin (laughing)

And I sing the ones that make you cry.

Harlequin (to Scaramouche)

I invite you to laugh at my funeral. (to Mezzetin) And I invite you to cry at my wedding. Now here it will be necessary to sing sad songs for the girls who are suffocated, and to sing merry songs about the girls who refuse to go in. Let's see if you know what to do.

Scaramouche (humming sadly)

Hem, hem, hem.

Harlequin

Joyous prelude.

Scaramouche (singing)

To the marriage of Jaques

Who came to celebrate—

Harlequin (mocking him)

Who comes to celebrate—hey, very well put.

Mezzetin (humming)

Hem, hem, hem.

Harlequin

That's what they call entering into the character—To declaim in tune! The sound agrees with the words. This man will make a new opera.

Scaramouche (singing)

To a man who was stabbed,

Then hanged after he was dead—

Harlequin

Haven't you got something else?

Mezzetin

Ah, ah, ah.

Harlequin

Sorry beginning.

Mezzetin

To be sure, sir, I have one that's very new. The heroic combat of a rooster and a hen. (singing)

We witness today a cruel fight.

Between a cock and a hen.

The angry hen

Bit the cock, the cock.

But a happy silence ensued.

The cock gave shout:

Cock a doodle doo,

What a how do you do.

The hen is happy

When the cock is singing.

(Exit Mezzetin and Scaramouche. Enter Octavio.)

Octavio

Sir, I am very much afflicted. I don't know what's become of my mistress. I saw her come in this side here. I still don't believe she was foolish enough to go in the Tree—for she was very prudent.

Harlequin

I'll tell you what. I'll read the epitaphs of those maidens who were suffocated by the Tree. See if you can recognize her.

Lucretia invites you to pity her fate

She killed herself in the arms of Tarquin

What a strange thing to do.

Octavio

I am too young to have loved Lucretia.

Harlequin

Passerby, regard my misfortune

In a moment a young thief ran in my door.

I tried to show him out.

I only opened to tell him

He couldn't come in.

And so he got in.

Who would have believed that!

Such a small oversight.

Alas, that for opening my door

I must suffer death. Was she your love?

Octavio

No, no. She never opened her door to me. I always came in the window.

Harlequin

Here lies the heroine of this village

Weak in love but very bold.

Through vanity she had found death in the Tree.

But of all the prudes of her time

She had the best of it.

She had joined the glorious reputation of being Chaste

To the pleasures of being wanton. Was she your love?

Octavio

No.

Harlequin

Here lies Aimee

Who died dancing the bournee.

She danced so wildly

She got the fidgets

And died of lack of respiration

Without even going in the Tree. Is this your mistress?

Octavio

No, my mistress doesn't know how to dance.

Harlequin

Here lies a maiden who thought she was chaste.

She restricted her love to simple bantering,

Or, so she said. To a hundred innocent games.

And to prove her chastity—she went under the Tree.

And now she's dead, you see. Was this your mistress?

Octavio

No, sir. My mistress never made jokes. She was always in earnest.

Harlequin

There no epitaph on that tomb there.

Old Woman (seated on the tomb)

Alas, I am the epitaph.

Harlequin

Well, I believe you weren't made of marble in your youth.

Old Woman

I intend to spend the rest of my life on this tomb, so I can inform all the passersby of the virtue of my daughters.

Harlequin

Inform me first.

Old Woman (descending from the tomb)

I am very unfortunate! I had only thirty daughters, and five are buried here in one tomb.

Harlequin

Seems to me, you are very fortunate. Apparently the five dead ones were not very chaste. They would have spoiled the other twenty-five. And, in fact, they proved the others were innocent. There are many large cities that cannot furnish that number.

Old Woman

Ah, the five deceased died by accident, and it was from natural feeling.

Harlequin

Natural feelings are the most tender. Tell me your story.

Old Woman

Here, sir. As I was walking here.

Harlequin

With your thirty daughters?

Old Woman

Yes, sir, with my little family. The youngest went to play in the Tree. As soon as she entered, she fell into a faint. Then one of her sisters went after her from natural feeling. She, too, fell into a faint, and then a third—

Harlequin

From natural feeling?

Old Woman

With two others and the fourth followed.

Harlequin

From natural feeling?

Old Woman

I ran quickly to prevent the fifth from entering. Alas, I arrived a little too late. What a shame it would be if I hadn't had more children. For they are—

Harlequin

So filled with natural feeling. (to Octavio) Well, friend, your mistress was good-natured and had natural feeling?

Octavio

No, sir. My mistress had neither sister, nor brother, nor mother, nor relative, and she was going to marry me just so she could have some relations.

Harlequin

Since your mistress isn't here, I must continue the Ceremony.

Our Tree is going to open—

This old stump will serve as a touchstone

To distinguish true gold from fool's gold.

If here there is someone pure

Without mixing or alloy

That comes to find in this hollow

A certificate of purity

She will be rewarded.

But if someone has the audacity

To approach here full of vanity

And void of fidelity

I pity the poor boasting virgin

Who thinks to triumph over this Tree.

Already I shiver,

For the Sacred Tree

Will suffocate 'er.

(Harlequin opens the Tree. Mezzetin comes out dressed as a peasant girl and faints.)

Octavio

There she is! That's my mistress. Why did she hide herself in the Tree without telling me?

Harlequin

You will learn this isn't the first stupidity she's been guilty of without informing you.

(The Farmer and Pierrot carry Mezzetin upstage and put Mezzetin down.)

Octavio

Damn. For the little she's given me, she shouldn't be dead.

Harlequin

Dead is dead.

Octavio

She was always subject to the vapors.

Harlequin

Cure her then, cure her if you can.

Octavio

If I had pee from the Queen of Hungary, I could cure her of any type of vapors.

Mezzetin (breathing)

Ah, ouf! It's because you cured me that the Tree suffocated me. (falling back) I am dead.

Octavio

She isn't dead.

Harlequin

Perhaps she only fainted.

Octavio

Maybe the Tree only punishes in proportion to the evil

done. I swear to you, I only kissed her hard.

Harlequin

That shouldn't lead to a faint these days.

Mezzetin

It's because I'm delicate. (falling back) Ah! Ouf!

Octavio

She's coming around, I tell you.

Harlequin

That's easy to see. (to Mezzetin) Did you give in?

Mezzetin

I don't know what you're talking about. Ah, ouf!

Octavio

Come, courage. She's coming back, sir—because when I took her hand, she wasn't paying any heed.

Harlequin

Most don't pay any heed. She could have consented without thinking. Consent is quicker than thought.

Mezzetin (getting up and singing)

Ah, ah, ah, ah.

Ah, what a great escape.

I wanted to prove my virtue.

I counted on it.

But it failed.

Ah, ah, ah, what a great escape.

Few girls like me

Prove true blue

If they are put in the Tree.

How lucky I was to escape.

Harlequin

For this once, the Tree pardons you.

(Octavio and Mezzetin exit arm in arm. Enter Catos with a baby in her arms.)

Catos (singing to the baby)

La, la, la, la.

Harlequin

Hey, it's my cousin Catos! What the devil brings you here? And where'd you get the baby? Ah, I understand. You bring this little girl here to test her chastity! She will always be able to say the Tree certified her. Very clever idea, cousin. No risk at all.

Catos

No, you're wrong. I came here to test myself in the Tree.

Harlequin

But, Catos, consider—

Catos

You're right—you're right—

Harlequin

You—you're very wrong.

Catos

To hell with the other girls in this village. I'm going to trap the Tree.

Harlequin

It will be the Tree that traps you.

Catos (aside)

The Tree won't dare to shut out a little creature like this. I'm sure she's pure enough for the two of us. I wouldn't be so stupid as to go in without her, cousin.

Harlequin

You speak a part. Is some remorse bothering you? Are you reminded of something?

Catos

It's nothing—pish.

Harlequin

Oh, remember pish and push?

Catos

Pish—pish, that's all.

Harlequin

It takes no more than a pish to wrong an honest girl.

Catos

Not so much cackling. Put me in the Tree, I want to go through with the Ceremony.

Harlequin

You're so ready. But, perhaps it will be a funeral ceremony.

Catos

Hey, hurry up. I am dancing already to make the scandalmongers shut up.

Harlequin

Do you remember what I said to you that day I found you crying by the fountain?

Catos

That was the day I lost a little—acorn.

Harlequin

You don't cry over losing a little acorn. You lost something else with it.

Catos

Oh, not much with it.

Harlequin

But, the other day, you were lost in the woods, and I put you on the right road.

Catos

I prefer that none of that be true. You are going to see that I will enter the Tree with my head held high.

Harlequin

The business is evident. But, if you absolutely wish to risk the boat—give the little girl to someone else to take care of.

Catos (hotly)

I'll take care of her. She's safe with me.

Harlequin

Better if you left her.

Catos

What, me leave this little runt! I love her too much.

Harlequin

Catos, Catos, I see your trickery. You believe you can hide behind the diapers of this pure little girl and get away with it. But you deceive yourself. In the case of virtue the strong protects the weak—and I believe you've been wilder than this baby has been chaste.

Catos

What! The Tree will suffocate this sweet little baby?

Harlequin

Assuredly.

Catos

She's an only child—and if something happened—I am going to take her to her mother.

(Exit Catos. All the players return.)

Harlequin

Come rare phoenix of village girls

Who wish to appear very chaste.

You will make your pretty friends jealous

By appearing alone as pure and chaste before all eyes.

To do that is to accuse the others of weakness.

Tremble in approaching the Tree of Lucretia.

If there are some who fear to prove it today

But still wish to prove their chastity in proper form

Come back in a decade or two.

I'll wait for you under the Tree.

Jaqueline (to her father)

Ah, Daddy, you've come just in time. Take me away and hide me.

Harlequin

Oh, no, if you please. You must submit to the law.

Peasant

What's this daughter? You shame me! What's going on?

Columbine

Alas, the poor child.

Pierrot

She has—

Peasant

She has—

Harlequin

She has—now she will tell you herself. She let the cat get the cheese.

Jaqueline

I couldn't help it. It was a monstrous cat.

Pierrot

Sir, if the cat has skimmed the cream off the milk, find someone else who will eat the porridge, if you can. And you, Miss, wait for me under the Tree. I am going to hook up with Columbine.

Columbine (aside)

That's all I ask.

Harlequin

I pity her—and as no person will marry her after such a confession, I believe myself obligated to take her myself.

Peasant

I am very happy to be rid of the little bitch.

Octavio (singing to Jaqueline)

They say it is shameful

For village boys

To suffer a girl to be chaste.

Your virtue scares us

But your scheme makes us bold.

And you render us honor

By losing your reputation to us.

Columbine (singing)

When a young pussy

With an air of modesty

Needs only a little help

On the velvet path

Like a little kiss

The purest of prudes

Can bring the matter

To a successful end.

The matter is delicate

But no one fears—

The matter is delicate—

My word it's such a little thing

One ought to leave it to the cat.

Harlequin

Certainly no one can refuse the cat.

Chorus

The cat, the cat, the cat, the cat—

What's the use of getting angry

When the little pussy

Has taken all the cream?

Such a delicate morsel.

When the little minx

Come purring and flattering

Better cry out—

The cat, the cat, the cat.

Harlequin

It is time to prove her innocence.

Jaqueline

If I'm married to Harlequin, I don't care what anybody says about me.

Harlequin

But, I care, as now your honor is mine. Gentlemen, please understand that the cheese the cat ate was real cheese. Cream cheese. Brie, as a matter of fact.

Jaqueline

What do you mean?

Harlequin

And to prove her chastity, I am going to put her in the Tree right now.

(Harlequin puts Jaqueline in the Tree.)

Pierrot

I smell a trick.

Jaqueline (singing)

I am the most chaste in my village.

My mother told me

And I believe her

That any girl who argued about it

Could come under the Tree with me.

(Now several girls want to go to the Tree, but the men prevent them.)

Harlequin (holding on to Catos as he sings)

There's nothing so tempting

As arguing about it.

But a prudent girl

Ought not to endanger her life.

Content yourself with dancing

And singing under the Tree.

Catos (singing)

I swear that I am pure.

My oath ought to be believed.

No one can prove a thing.

But if you want me to formally prove it—

Wait for me under the Tree.

Octavio (singing)

Margret, what madness

To put yourself in a Tree.

The law says you will lose your life

But I want you for my wife.

Still, you ought to die—I really should let you

Because so many times you've told me

—Wait for me under the Tree.

Chorus of Girls

A girl who's a little light

May die without resurrection.

But me, I've learned about love

And without dying

I can have a rendezvous

Under the Tree.

Harlequin (to the audience)

If the play pleased you, we beg your applause. If not, we'll close up shop. And while we're waiting, give us your money. Then wait for us under the trees.

CURTAIN

WAIT FOR ME UNDER THE ELM

CAST OF CHARACTERS

Lovelace

Polly

Jeremy

Lucy

Bellamy

Jacob

Lettice

Peter

Luke

THE PLAY

Jeremy

Let me put it in the plainest terms: I advanced the money for our expenses from our garrison to this village. We've already lived for fifteen days off my pile. Please settle up, and let me take my leave.

Lovelace

Oh—damn it. You pick a fine time.

Jeremy

Hey, sir, what better time is there? You've just been discharged. Now you must discharge your followers.

Lovelace

Jeremy, to quit an officer's service is to jeer at Fortune.

Jeremy

Sir, I've been jeered at since the day I entered your service—but, thank you very much, I am above

Fortune. I intend to retire from the world.

Lovelace

The stupid—stupid—

Jeremy

Yes, sire, I have made several little reflections on the vanity of worldly pleasures. I am tired of being beaten and malnourished. I am tired of spending my evenings at the door of a gambling den, and my days warning off whores. I am tired of whiling away the time at the buffet while you get drunk at the table. One must make an end, sir. I am going to marry a certain Lucy, who is the wittiest girl in this village. The prettiest girls in Wales consult her like an oracle because she understudied a coquette in London. It was in London that she became amorous of me.

Lovelace

Hey, why haven't I met this amiable Lucy? My star is running out of luck.

Jeremy

It's not your star, sir, it's my care in hiding Lucy from you. She's too pretty to make your acquaintance. But this digression is causing you to forget a little question of arithmetic between us. I've been in your service for eight years at twenty-five shillings per annum, sum total six hundred pounds; instead, I have received two hundred blows with your cane and fifty kicks in the ass: there remains then, the six hundred pounds, which I beg you to give me instantly.

Lovelace (in a rage)

What! I've had the patience to put up with a rascal like you for eight years!

Jeremy

A little more, actually.

Lovelace

A thief.

Jeremy

Yes, sir.

Lovelace

Eight years—a valet worth hanging!

Jeremy

Ah!

Lovelace

Who should be destroyed, wiped out!

Jeremy

Something's wrong here. Up to the present moment, you've been very satisfied with my service. The moment I ask for my wages, you change.

Lovelace (softening)

Jeremy, I am not to be duped by my own good nature today. Go, old boy, I have no intent of running you off.

Jeremy

Truly, sir, it's not you who is running me off. It's I who ask for my leave—and six hundred pounds.

Lovelace

No, dear heart, you cannot leave me. You know you are necessary to me. Rustic life does not agree with an intriguer, a trickster.

Jeremy

I know I have all the necessary talents to make my fortune in the city—but, I sacrifice my ambitions to Lucy—to whom I intend to give my six hundred pounds. Here, I'll give you a receipt. (pulls out a paper and gives it to Lovelace)

Lovelace

Plague on the cad! You have only your own business on your mind. Let's speak a little of mine. Tomorrow, I will marry Polly. I have managed things so well that her father is, at present, fonder of me than of his daughter. She has ten thousand pounds, Jeremy.

Jeremy

You've only got your own affairs in mind. Let's return a bit to mine.

Lovelace

Polly is waiting for me at her home at four o'clock. And before going to her, I have to arrange certain things with the solicitor.

Jeremy

Sir, there's only two words to my affair.

Lovelace

The notary is waiting for me, Jeremy.

Jeremy

My discharge and my wages.

Lovelace

Oh, if you absolutely insist on finishing our relationship together—

Jeremy

If it were not for a pressing circumstance—

Lovelace

One must make an effort.

Jeremy

I don't want to importune you.

Lovelace

You don't know how this pains me.

Jeremy

Here's your receipt.

Lovelace (taking the receipt and hugging Jeremy)

Go, I give you your leave.

Jeremy

And my wages?

Lovelace

You'll have to wait, Jeremy. I don't have time to see you anymore.

(Exit Lovelace.)

Jeremy

The rogue! I owe him one! Lucy has asked me to help break his engagement to Polly. Well, we'll see what we can do.

(Enter Lucy.)

Jeremy

Ah, you here!

Lucy

I've been looking for you for over an hour. Have you come to terms with your master?

Jeremy

Hardly. There's a dispute between him and me over two articles. I asked for my leave and my wages. He split the difference—he gave me my leave and kept my wages.

Lucy

And you refuse to take off the kid gloves with him? Do you still have to be pulled by the ear to help me break his marriage, to help my poor brother Bellamy to whom Polly was originally promised? It's up to you to make the whole village happy. There were dances and feasts held in honor of Bellamy and Polly, until this discharged officer came and stole the heart of the pretty farmer's daughter. And since then, all the gallants are in mourning.

Jeremy

I don't lack the will to do it, but I consider.

Lucy

And I, I consider nothing. I am very stupid to beg you when I have a right to command. Bellamy is my brother—and if he doesn't marry Polly as I wish, Lucy will not marry Jeremy.

Jeremy

Listen to that. You really put me in a predicament.

Lucy

Except that I am not like most women who create such dilemmas. I haven't given any deposit, and I will break it off if—

Jeremy

Easy. What has to be done for little brother Bellamy? Have you made any plans with him?

Lucy

Plans with Bellamy! He's a naïve young lover who is capable only of fidgeting. He comes, he goes, he can't sit still; he curses his unfaithful lover, and he always has some childish plan which he insists you listen to. Besides, he's a little obstinate—so, I've had to shut him up so he'll leave me in peace to manage his business. I believe that he's coming now.

(Enter Bellamy.)

Lucy

What! Little imp, are you always underfoot?

Bellamy

I crawled out of the window of the room you locked me up in, so as to come tell you that this plan of yours about a widow to expose Lovelace won't work.

Lucy

You'll be the death of me if you—

Jeremy

Let Bellamy speak. He seems like a weighty fellow to me.

Bellamy

Exactly. I discovered a secret that proves Polly loves me, and I began to think—

Lucy

So, go finish your thinking and leave me along to manage—

Bellamy

Oh—perhaps I could—

Lucy

It won't be you—

Bellamy

I tell you that—

Lucy

I tell you to quiet down—

Bellamy

Look, I'm the one who's in love. I want to talk—to speak—with all my soul.

Lucy

Oh—this little amorous troublemaker.

Bellamy

Hold on. If Jeremy tells me, I don't know better than you how to get Polly back—I'll return to my room.

Lucy

Let's listen, on that condition.

Bellamy

What I have here is a trick to get Polly in a corner while you both listen.

Jeremy

So far, so good.

Bellamy

And then, when she's there, I will say to her: "Since there's nobody who can hear us—isn't it true, Polly, that you've told me a hundred times that you love me?"

She'll say: "Yes, Bellamy, because it's true." I'll say: "Isn't it true that when you told me you loved me, I said that oaths were nice, but they don't mean anything. They don't prove you won't marry somebody else, besides me?" Polly will say: "Yes, Bellamy." Then I will say, "Isn't it true that on a certain day, when your collar pin broke, I repaired it sweetly, very sweetly?"

Lucy

Oh! Hurry up. I like dispatch.

Jeremy

This story is very promising. And we will be hidden to hear all this?

Bellamy

Right. I'm not going to hem and haw with her—for she's engaged to me and that covers everything—and if not, I'm quite easy that everyone knows who brought the earth to harvest. Anyway, then—I say to her: "Isn't it true that while opening your collar, I found a paper against your breast, and that on this paper you had written your name with mine to show that we would become one?" And she will say: "Yes, Bellamy." Oh, she may have gone to sleep by then, but I know she's only pretending, for I woke her once when—

Lucy

All right, now, after she's said all that?

Bellamy

You will jump out of your hiding place and say to her: "Polly, you must not marry anyone except Bellamy, or else we'll tell everybody that you love two men at the same time." She wouldn't put up with that.

Lucy

Oh, yes she would. Women love to glory in it.

Bellamy

To glory in loving someone else when one is already engaged! No—no, there isn't a woman like that in the whole world.

Jeremy

Bellamy hasn't been around. Still, I believe Mr. Bellamy is better at thinking than we are; however, we're better at doing than Bellamy. So—he is condemned to return to his chamber until we have need of him.

Bellamy

Oh, he cannot mean what he said, Lucy, because—hey!

Lucy (pushing him out)

Come on, go—or I'm not going to bother myself with your affairs.

Bellamy (exiting)

I'm going, but I'm furious.

Lucy

Oh, at last we are rid of him. Now all we have to do is cure Polly of her infatuation with your master.

Jeremy

Huh! When love gets into a heart as simple as Polly's, it's difficult to drive out. It's more firmly placed there than in the heart of a changeable coquette.

Lucy

I admit your master's grand airs have taken her imagination, but in the depths of her heart, she's still for Bellamy. Let's finish this up. We must prevent Polly from leaving home, so she cannot thwart our plans. How do you feel about it?

Jeremy

Hum! Listen, we've accustomed her to London fashions. Suppose I told her my master wanted her to have presentable clothes. The hairdressing alone would keep an ordinary woman busy all day long.

Lucy

Here she comes. Think of a way to keep her here.

Polly (entering)

Jeremy, where's your master? I've been waiting for him for two hours.

Jeremy

You're mistaken, Madame, my master is very intent on your waiting for him.

Lucy (aside to Polly)

Didn't I tell you his zeal wouldn't last?

Polly

Oh, on the contrary, Lucy, Lovelace must be in love with me today to utter madness, for he promised me that each day his love would grow; and he's already loved me since yesterday.

Lucy

In one night, a man's heart may undergo a revolution.

Jeremy

Yes, at the end of this century, loves, like the seasons, are quite out of cycle; hot and cold come only by caprice.

Lucy

In this village, we have an absolute rule: it's that on the wedding day the thermometer of tenderness is in a very high degree; but the next day it drops a bit.

Polly

You both want to convince me that Lovelace will be inconstant—but, I'd have to be crazy to believe that he would change. What! When Bellamy told me quite simply that he would be faithful to me forever, I believed him—and you expect me not to believe Lovelace, who is a refined gentleman, and who takes the most horrible oaths that he will love me always?

Jeremy

In love, the oaths of a lover mean nothing; it's the language of the country.

Lucy

If you would listen to me one time in your life, I would make you see that Lovelace—

Polly

Let's talk about something else, shall we, Lucy—

Jeremy

She's right. (to Polly) Let's talk about the beautiful clothes my master is going to get for you.

Polly

Oh, Jeremy, I'm delighted!

Jeremy

By the way, my master would like you to dress today in London fashion.

Polly

I'd like nothing better myself, but I don't know which of my two clothes I should wear. Tell me, Jeremy, which does he like better, the ingénue or the seductress?

Jeremy

The harlot/seductress has always been to my master's taste.

Polly

London women must have great wit to invent such

clever names.

Jeremy

The devil! Their imagination works overtime. They only invent fashions to hide sins. Furbelows for those who don't have hips; those who have hips, hide them. The long neck and wrinkled throat have given place to the steinkerk and so forth.

Polly

What puzzles me the most is the coiffure. I can never arrange so much machinery on my head. There's never room to put half of it.

Jeremy

Oh—when it's a question of arranging pieces of nonsense, the head of a woman has more understanding than one gives them credit for. But, you remind me that I have here an instruction book on the coiffure translated from the French and direct from London. It's entitled: "The Elements of the Toilet, or the Harmonious System of Feminine Coiffure."

Polly

Oh! How nice that book must be!

Jeremy (drawing the book from his pocket)

Here's the second volume. The first only contained an alphabetical list of the principal pieces used, like: La Duchess, le solitaire, Les Fontages, le chou, la tête-à-tête, la culbute, the somersault, Le Mousquetaire, le firmament, the tenth heaven, the palissade, and the mouse.

Polly

Ah, Jeremy, find the place in the book which describes the Mouse. I have a knot of ribbon called "le souris."

Jeremy

Here's some of it; listen: "Coiffure to shorten the face."— That's not it. "Dashing little curls for straight faces and long noses." I'm not there yet. "Ingenious supplements which give relief to flat cheeks." Listen to that! "Flying headpieces to make the eyes stand out." Ah, here's what you ask: "The Mouse—a little ribbon of silk which is placed in the wood. Note: one calls 'wood' a little pack of bristling hairs which garnish the front of a wooden buckle." But, you can read this at your leisure. Go quickly, arrange your toilet. I will send my master to you as soon as he has finished some business he has.

Polly

He won't have to wait for me, at least. Adieu, Lucy.

Lucy

Adieu, Polly.

(Exit Polly.)

Lucy

It's apparent that in the end, in this world, each must be deceived through his weakness: men by women, women by their clothes.

Jeremy

He's with the notary. He'll have to pass this way to see Polly, and I will delay him while you go disguise yourself as the widow.

Lucy

Go over this disguise a little. You're certain your master has never seen this widow?

Jeremy

Assuredly. My boasting is based on her reputation in the county of being very rich; that she is in love with him. To revenge herself on him for his indifference, she's taken pleasure in appearing masked at two or three parties where he was—to inflame him—in a word, to mock him, always finding an excuse for not unmasking. She's a merry widow, who plays a thousand pranks like this to liven up her widowhood.

Lucy

Since it's that way, I'll counterfeit the widow better than she herself could.

Jeremy

So be it. One cannot know how to play the woman if you don't know how to play a married woman.— Is the dress ready?

Lucy

Yes.

Jeremy

Here comes my master.

Lucy

Amuse the gallows bird, so I can disguise myself— then go warn Polly, so that she may come and surprise us.— You will make her eavesdrop on our conversation. Let me proceed.

(Exit Lucy.)

Jeremy

Now, how shall I bring it off? But, one doesn't need much skill with my master. A man who believes himself loved by the ladies is easily duped.

(Enter Lovelace.)

Jeremy

Sir, sir!

Lovelace

Don't stop me. Polly is waiting for me.

Jeremy

There's more to my business than I expect to speak to you about at present.

Lovelace

I'm dying with impatience to see her. Love, Jeremy, love— Ah, when one's heart is taken.

Jeremy

I had never thought you to be the type of man to let love prevent him from making his fortune.

Lovelace

What do you mean by that?

Jeremy

That your love for Polly would make you lose this widow of fifty thousand pounds.

Lovelace

Hey! Didn't you say this crazy woman has become invisible?

Jeremy

Apparently, she intends to test your fidelity. The happy moment is come. She is here.

Lovelace

Is it possible?

Jeremy

Nothing could be more true—and since you have left me— But let's not speak of it any more—your heart belongs to Polly.

Lovelace

Finish, Jeremy, finish.

Jeremy

In love, as you are, you wouldn't break off a marriage of inclination for a difference of twenty thousand pounds more or less.

Lovelace

One would have to employ violence. But, with twenty thousand pounds, one could buy a regiment; one is useful to the King—you know, a man of honor ought to sacrifice himself to the interests of his country.

Jeremy

Between us, the country has no great need of you—it's already thanked you for your services.

Lovelace

Speak of the widow, Jeremy.

Jeremy

The widow came to town this morning to see your handsome face. And, after you left me, she offered me a hundred pounds if I would deliver your heart to her.

Lovelace

Jeremy, old friend, faithful servant, I'd be delighted to help you earn a hundred pounds. I love to pay my obligations, Jeremy.

Jeremy

By reducing my wages and paying them off with hers!

Lovelace

What does it take, dear heart?

Jeremy

It's agreed between us, that chance will bring the widow under this elm tree in a quarter of an hour.

Lovelace

Excellent.

Jeremy

I have promised her that the same chance will bring you there.

Lovelace

Dear Jeremy.

Jeremy

You must walk up and down without seeming to do anything. She's going to come without seeming to do anything. You will accost her without seeming to; she will listen to you without seeming to. That's how marriages are made in London.

Lovelace

My word, you're an adorable man.

Jeremy

There—prepare to accost the widow like a schoolmaster. Hide an eye with your hat, hand on your belt, elbow sticking out, body to the side, head the other way—and be careful not to walk a straight path. That's a good little bourgeois.

Lovelace

You rascal, you know almost as much as I do.

Jeremy

Now's the time, sir, to profit by the talents you have acquired in the grand art of trickery! Ah, if you recall that glance you gave the other day at the theatre—a certain glance that caused a woman you had never spoken to in your life to lose her reputation.

Lovelace

You're a jokester.

(Enter Lucy, dressed as the widow.)

Jeremy (low to Lovelace)

Here's the widow, sir. Pretend to do nothing. (aloud to Lovelace, while signaling to Lucy) Is there nothing new in the catalogue? Have you received letters from London? The promenade is awfully deserted today. Which way's the wind blowing? My God—pretty day!

Lovelace (low to Jeremy)

Jeremy, the poor thing is sighing.

Jeremy (low to Lovelace)

Apparently, for the deceased.

Lovelace

We have to let her suffer a little more. She's sensitive to music. I'll use that to my advantage.

Jeremy

Right. Your style is full of merit, and you have even more wit. If she listens to your song, she'll be charmed, sir. Don't you remember some impromptu from the latest opera?

Lovelace

I am going to sing to keep from being bored—a little air that I composed for a charming widow. (singing)

Damn—love is stupid.

Yes, stupid.

Without regard for my birth

Love makes me sigh.

Love makes me tremble.

Just like a bourgeois.

Damn—love is stupid.

There's no prettier face in England.

Must I submit to this pretty flirt?

And in recompense

Be enchained

Like a galley slave?

Damn—love is stupid.

Jeremy (after Lovelace finishes his song)

You are love itself, sir.

Lovelace (low to Jeremy)

It's enough to make one expire. Heavens, what an adventure, Jeremy. I believe that now my amiable invisible is going to speak to me.

Jeremy

It's herself.

Lovelace (accosting her)

By what chance, Madame, do you find yourself in this village?

Lucy

I came to seek out solitude and cry if I want to.

Jeremy

Let us retire, sir; it is dangerous to interrupt the tears of a widow. The sight of a handsome man reopens the wound.

Lovelace

I have told you a hundred times, charming, spiritual

Lady, I am the English Cavalier most specific for the consolation of ladies. I am the remedy.

Lucy

A knight like you cannot console one—without afflicting many others.

Lovelace

Let all the women in the world perish of jealousy, provided you desire—

Lucy

Ah! Don't finish, sir. I fear you're about to make proposals to me that I cannot listen to without horror. My husband has only been dead eight years.

Lovelace

Ah, Jeremy, I sense my flame reigniting.

Jeremy

She is speaking of the deceased. Your affair is going well.

Lucy

My husband made me promise when he died, (lowering her voice) that I must never remarry.

Jeremy

Profit by the opportunity, sir. She's a woman, and when she lowers her voice, it means she's weakening.

Lucy (stammering)

I w-will k-keep my p-promise—and y-yet—

Jeremy (low to Lovelace)

She's stammering. Time for me to retire.

Lovelace (low to Jeremy)

Go on, then.

(Exit Jeremy.)

Lovelace

You are alone, Madame. Do for me now what you have always refused to do—raise your cruel veil.

Lucy

Sir, sorrow has so changed me.

Lovelace

Hey, I pray you—

Lucy (in an affected tone)

I never sleep. Fatigue causes wrinkles. The heat—the dust—I'm afraid you'll think I'm ugly.

Lovelace

I will find you charming. (aside) You'd have to be uglier than Medusa to frighten me off, child.

Lucy (raising her veil)

You mean it?

Lovelace

What do I see?

Lucy

I suppose it's necessary to admit that from the second time I saw you, I intended to make your fortune—but I had to test you. Ah! Cruel man—did you have to rebuff me so soon?

Lovelace

Hey—where have I seen you, Madame?

(Enter Jeremy, leading Polly to listen.)

Polly (aside to Jeremy)

Is it for this that you made me wait?

Jeremy (aside)

Listen.

(Exit Jeremy.)

Lovelace

I admit frankly, that because of your refusal I lowered my sights to a farmer's daughter—because I found a pile of money to compensate for the great wealth I might have had from you.— But, honor bright, I never regarded her as anything but a child, a doll to play with, and since our charming conversation in London, you have never lost the empire you gained over my heart.

Polly (aside)

The traitor!

Lucy

Evidently, I believe you, for I still intend to marry you. But above all, you must first tell this Polly, in her presence, that you never loved her.

Lovelace

In her presence?

Lucy

What, do you hesitate?

Lovelace

Not at all. But, how can I say to a woman, face to face, that I don't love her? It would kill her. The blow is mortal, Madame, and I ought to have some care of a poor creature who—

Lucy

Who?

Lovelace

Who? To tell you a secret has a certain weakness for me—but, I am a gallant man.

Polly (aside, agitated)

How he lies!

Lovelace

But, Madame, I will give up all to follow you. I let myself be caught. I will marry you. Is more proof of my love necessary?

Lucy

At least, I order you to break the engagement you have with her father, immediately.

Lovelace

Oh, as to that, willingly.

Lucy

Go, promptly, and return in half an hour—and wait for me here—under the elm.

Lovelace

I will give you satisfaction.

Lucy

Under the elm—remember.

(Exit Lovelace.)

Polly (not daring to accost the widow)

I must know it from her. But, dare I meet her after what he just told her about me?

Lucy

My God! The pretty trollop. How lovely. Do you wish to speak to me?

Polly

No.

Lucy

I believe I've seen you somewhere. Aren't you the pretty Polly, the farmer's daughter?

Polly

I don't know.

Lucy

Don't be afraid, my little sweetheart. You stole my lover from me—but I've already avenged myself, because he as sacrificed you to me.

Polly

The traitor.

Lucy

You're angry, aren't you, to lose such a handsome little man?

Polly

I'm angry that he told you lies about me. He said that I had a weakness for him. Ah, don't believe that, Madame, he's a bad man, and will say the same of you.

Lucy

Ha, ha.

Polly

You laugh? Is it because you believe what that liar told you?

Lucy

Lovelace doesn't know how to lie; he is a gentleman.

Polly

How unhappy I am! What! You believe him?

Lucy (unveiling)

Yes, I do.

Polly

It's Lucy.

Lucy

I believe him the way I've always believed him—and I believe that you are very wise and Lovelace is a rat. But, I am happy you listened. You see, it's not his fault that I am a phony widow. Well, what does your heart say now?

Polly

I am betrayed. Does Bellamy still love me?

Lucy

He will always love you if you love him. And if you say one word to him, he will devote his life to paying Lovelace back.

Polly

Ah! That's not bad: Lovelace told me he was no good.

Lucy

It's an act of vengeance that will serve to divert all our fashionable society. Lovelace will be bantered to such a degree that he will have his fill of it.

(Enter Bellamy.)

Bellamy (aside, without seeing Polly)

Jeremy just told me all that's happening to make me patient. But, although I may spoil everything, I cannot hold still. I'm too much in love.

Polly (angry to have been betrayed to Bellamy)

Ah, Bellamy, Bellamy.

Bellamy (seeing her)

At least I didn't say I was in love with you! It would be very silly for me to still love an ingrate.

Polly

That's true.

Bellamy

An infidel!

Polly

Yes, Bellamy.

Bellamy

A changeable woman.

Polly

Alas, I didn't want to change—it just happened—'cause I had never seen a man like Lovelace before.

Bellamy

Oh, yes. You are a traitress.

Polly

Oh—as for being a traitor—I didn't avoid you when I fell in love with Lovelace.

Bellamy (stifling, from a lover's rage)

Ah—ouf! There's but one way I can return to my old self. Give me your hand.

Polly

Ah, Bellamy—how angry I am.

Bellamy

Ah, Polly—how good I feel.

Lucy

You will use up all your tenderness—keep it for after you get married—then you'll need it. Now, Lovelace is coming to wait for me under the elm. We've resolved to mock him—Peter, Jacob, and Luke are going to aid us. They are already near. Here they are, in fact.

(Enter Jacob and shepherds.)

Lucy

Who told you it was already time?

Jacob

We saw from a distance that she let Bellamy kiss her hand.

Bellamy

It's the sign of the return of a lost spirit.

Polly

How ashamed I am, Jacob, to have been deceived by such a man.

Jacob

Alas, which one of us doesn't arrive at that point? But, we are going to make this little Lothario, Lovelace, see that he doesn't know his job, if he lets a girl have time to think.

Lucy

Are you ready in your roles to mock him?

Jacob

Exactly. Luke and Peter will make an opera of it in two hours.

Lucy

Yes, I am going to give you your parts.

Jacob

Here's Lovelace. Hide! It's time for me to begin.

(They all leave hurriedly. Enter Lovelace, going under the elm.)

Lovelace

Here we are a little beforehand. I haven't seen the girl or her father. If this widow plays me a little trick, it's going to be easy to go back to Polly—because I haven't left. I hear the villagers singing—let's let them pass by.

(Enter Jacob and Lettice. Lettice sings to a peasant boy who flees.)

Jacob

My poor Lettice, you're wasting your time and your song. It's true I've loved you, but it's exactly because of that that I don't love you anymore. Those are the rules.

Lettice (singing)

When you promised me

Under the fatal elm

That I would soon

Triumph over my rival

Ah! Why didn't I profit by it?

It wouldn't be so painful.

Now, I can only reproach your infidelity.

Jacob (singing)

It's true that my frankness

Was surprised by your deceiving talk

And your charming manners.

I wanted to do something stupid.

You didn't take me at my word.

You were the stupid.

You were the fool.

You were the chump.

Lovelace

These villagers are naturally gallant. But the widow's a little late.

(Enter Jeremy.)

Jeremy

Ah, sir—we've had bad luck.

Lovelace

What is it?

Jeremy

The widow's gone, sir. One of her aunts came to drag her away. All the poor woman could do was to stick her hand out of the carriage window and make me a sign that she would always love you.

Lovelace

Is she mocking me?

Jeremy

Sir, I've saddled your horse. He's tied up at the door. If you wish to follow, the carriage cannot have got far.

Lovelace

Jeremy, we have to do something we can be certain of. I am going to find Polly and conclude things with her. Here she is right now when I want her.

(Enter Polly.)

Polly (aside)

I am indeed going to mock him. (aloud) Ah, here you are, sir. I suppose I have to look for you all day?

Lovelace

Ah, pardon, my charmer. I had a business transaction that I couldn't put off.

Polly

Rather—weren't you being unfaithful?

Lovelace

What do you say, cruel unjust ingrate? May heaven witness—

Polly

Hey, don't swear. I know how much you love me.

Lovelace

But you—who speak of love—can love wait until tomorrow?

Polly

All right— Let's get married now!

Lovelace

Tell that to papa—to shorten the formalities, the articles, the contract.

Jeremy

A stupid custom for lovers who are in a hurry.

Polly

We will go in a moment to find my father—and if he makes us wait too long, we'll marry ourselves all by ourselves.

Chorus of farmers and shepherds from the depths of the theatre

If you wait for me under the elm

You may have to wait a while!

Lovelace

What's that I hear?

Polly

It's the wedding of a boy named Bellamy. Don't you know who he is?

Jeremy (leaping about)

A wedding! My word, I'm going to dance.

(Enter the shepherds.)

Lovelace

They're coming. Let's give them room.

Polly

Oh—I have to be of that party.

Lovelace

What—you can change in a minute?

Polly

As soon as the marriage is over, we can get married.

Chorus

Wait for me under the elm.

You may have to wait a while.

Lovelace

Jeremy, something funny's happening.

Jeremy

Pure chance, sir.

Lovelace

In that case, we must put a good face on it. (mingling with the villagers) Good, children. Long live the people of this village! Courage, Jeremy.

Chorus

Take the filly

At first chance

'Cause she's subject

To changes.

Often the most tender

When you make them wait

Mock you

At the rendezvous.

Jeremy (mocking Lovelace)

We are betrayed. They are mocking us, sir.

Lovelace

This confounds me.

Lucy (singing)

You, who have for heritage

Only your good looks

Neither money, nor equipage

You lack nothing.

Despite your discharge

The widow will do it.

Wait under the elm

—Perhaps, she'll come!

Polly (singing to Lovelace)

The village girl

Only gives to a soldier

A passing love.

It's the right of war.

But the formal contract

It's the peasant's lot.

Wait for me under the elm

Captain Good-for-Nothing.

Bellamy (singing)

One day

Our greedy cat

Caught a mouse.

But, because it was

Too delicate

Let it go

To catch a

RAT!

Jeremy (to Lovelace)

These are bad jokes, sir. Your horse is saddled.

(Lovelace starts to draw his sword.)

Peter

Gently, or we'll sound the tocsin on you.

Lovelace

I am going to sack this village with a regiment which I will purchase expressly for the purpose.

Lucy

From the widow's mite?

(Exit Lovelace in a fury. The villagers pursue Lovelace, singing.)

Chorus

Wait for me under the elm.

You may have to wait a long time!

CURTAIN

THE UNFORESEEN RETURN

CAST OF CHARACTERS

Mr. Edward Richly

Belinda

Clarissa

Squire

Lucy

Mrs. Prim

Roger

Jeremy

Mr. Andre

Mr. Richly

Six men, four women

THE PLAY

The scene is a street before Richly's house. Lucy, a maid, is approaching from one side and encounters Mrs. Prim.

Mrs. Prim:

Ah, there you are! I'm very glad to meet you. Let's take the opportunity to have a little serious conversation, Miss Lucy.

Lucy: (easily)

Just as serious as you please, Mrs. Prim.

Mrs. Prim:

You know perfectly well that I am displeased with the behavior of my niece.

Lucy:

Really Madam. And what's she done wrong, may I ask?

Mrs. Prim:

She does nothing but wrong—and to make it worse, she surrounds herself with a wench like you who gives her the worst possible advice and who pushes her over the precipice—where she's heading if she hasn't already fallen.

Lucy:

Well, Mrs. Prim, this is, at the very least, a serious conversation as you put it—and if I were to respond as seriously I don't know where it might end. But the respect I have for your age, and for the aunt of my mistress, prevents me from responding to you without respect.

Mrs. Prim:

My age! You're a model of moderation!

Lucy:

It would be nice if you were, too, Madam. You are not the first to spread scandal about your niece; remarks that have no foundation except in your disordered imagination.

Mrs. Prim:

My disordered imagination! What impudence. (furiously) It's the disorder of your actions which make me speak out—and there is nothing worse than the life you are living.

Lucy:

How is that—what's wrong with our life, if you please?

Mrs. Prim:

What? Is there anything more scandalous than the expenditures Belinda is constantly making—a girl without a penny in income.

Lucy:

You have credit, Madame.

Mrs. Prim:

Just what she needs to maintain a large house and extravagant tastes.

Lucy:

Is she forbidden to make her fortune?

Mrs. Prim:

And how is she to make her fortune?

Lucy:

Very innocently. She drinks, eats, sings, laughs, gambles, walks to take the air—and wealth comes to us while we sleep, I assure you.

Mrs. Prim:

And meanwhile her reputation evaporates. She'll learn. She won't have a penny of mine. My brother, who wanted her to be a nun, will disinherit her. Patience, patience, she won't always be young.

Lucy:

Very true, that's why we must put our time to good use.

Mrs. Prim:

Oh, very well—and all the profit you will get from that will be to die in a charity ward: both dishonored.

Lucy:

Oh, for that, no, Madam. A successful marriage will prevent that prophecy from being fulfilled.

Mrs. Prim:

A successful marriage. She's going to get married?

Lucy:

Yes indeed.

Mrs. Prim:

Just in time! But I won't be a party to it. I won't help her make anyone think she's either respectable or rich. I renounce her as my niece, and I will not aid her to deceive anyone; goodbye.

Lucy:

Don't trouble yourself—we know our business better than you.

Mrs. Prim:

I believe this will be some grand alliance!

(Exit Mrs. Prim in a huff)

Lucy:

This will be a fine marriage, and when it is consummated you will be honored to receive her and be her aunt.

(shouting after Mrs. Prim) You just wait and see! (Lucy is annoyed, stung by Mrs. Prim's remarks. She would like to say more, but cannot.)

Roger: (entering)

Good day, child. Who was that old lady you were talking with?

Lucy:

Who? That was Mrs. Prim, my mistress's aunt.

Roger:

I didn't recognize her. I wasn't paying much attention.

Lucy:

The old girl's very well off. She owns a lot of property in London. Belinda is very well connected, at least.

Roger:

But she hasn't any money of her own.

Lucy:

There's no reason to give up. Money will come. If her three uncles, two aunts, three cousins, and two nephews die—she will have a very large inheritance. Ha, ha! Do you know that if the Plague were to strike again, Belinda would cut quite a figure.

Roger:

She has a nice figure already.

Lucy:

Her beauty carries all before it.

Roger:

My master is absolutely determined to marry her.

Lucy:

And she is absolutely determined to marry him.

Roger:

There would perhaps be some trouble if our good father were to return—but he won't for a while. We'll have the time to prepare and my master will be happy—except for the chagrin of marrying Belinda.

Lucy:

What—what are you trying to say?

Roger:

Marriage is subject to its ups and downs.

Lucy:

You are very polite to think that Mr. Edward would ever repent of marrying Belinda, a young lady that I have brought up myself.

Roger:

So much the worse.

Lucy:

A pretty girl, young and well-developed.

Roger:

That part doesn't reassure me.

Lucy:

A girl easy to live with.

Roger:

Most girls are not hard to live with—at first.

Lucy:

A young lady who is wise and virtuous.

Roger: (wonderingly)

And you say you raised her?

Lucy: (furiously)

Why don't you go ahead and say what you want to say, wiseacre?

Roger:

Well, do you want me to speak openly? I don't like this alliance at all. And I foresee that it won't benefit anyone. Mr. Edward spends his money because he is in love, and love makes a man open-handed: marriage ruins love. If my master becomes a miser, where will we be?

Lucy:

He's of too prodigal a nature ever to turn miser. Has he given orders for today's feast?

Roger:

Let's see. Three cooks arrived with their set-ups. Leonard, the famous Leonard, marched at their head. The illustrious Florel has sent six bottles of Champagne—he made it himself.

Lucy:

So much the better. I love expensive stuff—but here is Mr. Edward.

(Edward Townley enters from the house. He is youthful,

open, and expensively dressed.)

Edward:

Ha! Good day, my dear Lucy—how are things with you, child? And how is your beautiful lady?

Lucy:

She's at home with Clarissa.

Edward:

Go, run, my dear Lucy: beg her to come here as soon as possible. I have no happy moments except those I pass with her.

Lucy:

You two are made for each other. When you're not around, she's bored to death. She won't delay, I promise you.

(Exit Lucy)

Roger:

Well, sir! You're really going to get married? Very soon you will have finished your love affair and your money. Not the best way to finish the business. But if you are going to do it, so be it. What will we tell your father when he returns from his business trip to Spain?

Edward:

You always have inopportune thoughts. Look, my friend: frolic in the present, have no regret for the past; and don't. whatever you do, read irritating portents in the future. That's the secret of happiness. By the way, haven't you received any money for me in the past few days?

Roger:

In the last three weeks I've obtained a half-year's rent on the farm in advance. In return, you've given Farmer Small a quittance for the entire year.

Edward:

Excellent!

Roger:

Last week I received 1,800 pounds for those two paintings your father refused to sell for thirty thousand.

Edward:

Fine!

Roger:

Fine! Also, I got 200 pounds for that tapestry your father purchased for five thousand two years ago.

Edward:

Better!

Roger:

Yes, yes, we've had a real white sale during his absence, haven't we?

Edward:

It's a little nourishment that we must take sometimes; and we will work together on more nourishment in the future.

Roger:

Work by yourself, because I have a bad conscience about being the instrument of your ruin. It's with my help you've been able to dissipate 10,000 pounds, not to mention another ten thousand you owe here and there to usurers and money lenders, who are just waiting to fall on us and gobble everything up when the day comes to pay them back.

Edward:

The one who disturbs me the most and causes me the most embarrassment is this Mr. Andre. He persecutes me, and I only owe him a hundred pounds!

Roger:

He isn't only after that. You also gave him a promissory note for 500 pounds. Four days ago he took out a judgment on the note. And it won't be pleasant if you spend your wedding night in jail.

Edward: (calmly)

We will find a way to deal with him.

Roger:

What way? We have no cash at all. All your income is taken in advance and spent as received. The townhouse furniture has been sold for a song—we've cut down the timber at the country house under the pretext of using it for fuel. As for me, I swear to you that I see no way out.

Edward:

If my father can be kept from returning another five or six months, I will have plenty of time to repair by my economy the expensive disorders of my youth.

Roger:

Assuredly. And your esteemed father, for his part—hasn't he worked hard to amass all this wealth?

Edward:

Without a doubt.

Roger:

It's better that you practice this foolishness while he's still alive. After he's dead, he won't be in a position to straighten things out.

Edward:

You're right, Roger.

Roger:

Sir, you're not so bad that you can't, at least, speak well. Your father will have made a huge profit from his trip—and you will have made a huge expenditure in his absence. Of what can he complain when he returns? It will be as if he had never gone, and at worst it will be his fault for having been so foolish as to make the trip.

Edward:

You're really talking some sense today, Roger.

Roger:

Between you and me, your father is not very bright. I've led him by the nose and you know it. I can make him believe anything I want to. And when he comes back this time, I think I still have power enough to pull you out of this sorry mess. Let's go, sir. Good cheer and a warm fire. Courage returns to me. How many for dinner tonight?

Edward:

Five or six.

Roger:

And your dear friend the self-styled Squire who has helped you to gobble up so much of your wealth so stylishly—will he be here?

Edward:

He promised me he would, but here is the charming Belinda and her cousin—

(Enter Belinda, Clarissa, and Lucy)

Belinda:

The precautions you make me take, Edward, can only be justified by the success they are having—and I will be entirely lost in worldliness if our marriage doesn't end all the pleasure parties I'm used to.

Edward:

I have never had any other sentiments, pretty Belinda—

and here is your friend who can bear witness to it.

Clarissa:

I guarantee the goodness of your heart if you must take this moment to justify yourself; but I, who never get mixed up in anything adventurous and who haven't seen the conclusion of this affair—what kind of role must I play—and what will people say of it, I pray?

Roger:

They'll say that people are known by the company they keep—and that the company made you get married. My master has so many friends—you have only to pick.

Lucy:

Take one, madame. The crazier things are—the more fun. Come on—make a choice!

Clarissa:

I'll marry the devil. Now that you mention it, I think I'll marry off Lucy—because of the company. It's a very contagious example.

Edward:

I wish you'd follow our example. I have a young friend who is alienated from his family. That's the way to recommend him. Has he told you of his feelings?

Clarissa:

No. This sort of marriage doesn't interest me. I don't follow anyone's lead. I want to take a husband as independent as I am.

Edward:

Well said. My friend isn't the type to let you put a bridle on him.

Roger:

But here is the Squire, who comes to see you. I am going to see if everything is ready for your supper.

(Exit Roger to the house)

Squire: (entering from the street)

Your servant, my friend. Ah, ladies, I am delighted to see you. You are waiting for me and that's very proper. I am the very soul of your parties, I admit. The premier mover in your pleasures, I know it. Where are we now? Is the supper ready? Are we getting married? Shall we abandon ourselves to wine? Come on, bring on the gaiety—I've never been in such a mood, in such spirits—I defy you to bore me.

Clarissa:

Truly, Squire, you were wise to wait.

Lucy:

It would be silly if a Squire were the first to come! One would think he had nothing to do.

Squire:

I assure you ladies that my coach cannot fly faster. It's less than three-quarters of an hour since I left Saint James. You know I usually use Arabian horses. There are simply no better horses for a quick rendezvous.

Edward:

What affair is so pressing?

Squire:

If we didn't have flying carriages like that, we'd miss half our opportunities.

Belinda:

And since when, Squire, are you mixed up with going to court? It seems that you ordinarily stay at Oxford.

Squire:

Well, what of it, my dear?

(To Edward)

Here you are awash in pleasure—you swim in delights. You know the interest that I take in all that concerns you. What happiness when two well-tested hearts approach the long-awaited moment—there one sees the ending of—a novel. This is a great day for you.

Edward:

I feel my happiness in all this talk.

(To Squire)

But tell me, I beg you, have you been, as you promised, to the jeweler for the diamonds?

Squire: (to Clarissa)

And you pretty cousin, what is it? Your heart says nothing to you? The example should encourage you—don't you wish, in marrying, to pay your debts to love and nature? It is terrible to be useless in this world.

Clarissa:

I am not bored yet with my virginity.

Squire:

Whenever you please, we will take the same momentous step—hearts united. I am made for the ladies, and, in all modesty, the ladies are made for me. May I be damned if you are not to my taste. I am ready to love you one day to the point of adoration—to the point of madness! But not to the point of marriage. I like amours without consequences—you understand me, I'm sure?

Lucy:

Truly, this speech is so plain it needs no commentary. What! Squire! For shame!

Squire:

You can't know how much this little fellow shames me. It is true this little bourgeois hasn't an equal, and that I treat him like family, introduce him into society, teach him to gamble, educate his taste in manners, furniture, and horses. I lead him a little astray—but these little gentlemen are not very happy unless one inspires them with the manners of the court, and they learn to ruin themselves in two or three years.

Lucy:

Have you many scholars?

Squire:

Where is Roger? I don't see him here. He's a pretty fellow. I love him. I find him admirable as a trickster, to keep off creditors, to calm usurers, to persuade and pacify merchants. To sell all the furniture in a house quietly and quickly. How fashionable, how witty of your father, how prudent, to leave you a governor so wise, an economist so knowing. This rogue values twenty thousand pounds rent the same way a baby does a half penny.

(Enter Roger)

Roger:

Ladies and gentlemen, when you wish to enter, supper is ready.

Squire:

Yes. Well said. We mustn't lose time. I told you that Roger was a pretty fellow. I feel in a praiseworthy mood to drink wine. You will see if I remain in that mood. Come ladies—those who love me—follow me.

Edward:

Moments are very precious to lovers. Let's not lose any time.

(Exit all but Roger into the house)

Roger:

Well, thank God, business is good, our lovers are happy. May Heaven make it last a long while! But what do I see? There, I believe comes Jeremy, the valet of our absent master.

(Enter Jeremy)

Jeremy:

At last I'm home. Hey, good day, Roger—the prodigal returns. How are you?

Roger:

And you—dreadful apparition, how are you?

Jeremy:

As you see, couldn't be better. A little tired, but we had a very successful trip.

Roger:

What! "We" had a very successful trip? You didn't come alone?

Jeremy:

What a question. Of course not. Came with my master. He went to the customs house with the merchandise while I came with the personal baggage and the joyous news for his son that he is returned in perfect health.

Roger:

News like that will certainly rejoice him.

(Low)

What are we going to do?

Jeremy:

Something wrong? You don't look well—and you don't seem very glad to see us.

Roger:

I'm not. This is most troublesome. All is lost. Now tell me—will he be kept at the custom house long?

Jeremy:

No—he'll be here any minute.

Roger:

Any minute? I think I'll go nuts.

Jeremy:

But what the hell's the matter with you?

Roger:

I don't know. Oh, the cursed old man. To return at such a bad time—and not to forewarn us. What a treacherous bastard.

Jeremy:

You must be up to something deep; this unexpected return hasn't upset your plans too much, has it?

Roger:

Oh, no! They'll all mixed up—by all the devils in hell!

Jeremy:

Too bad.

Roger:

Jeremy, my poor, Jeremy, help me to arrange things, I beg you.

Jeremy:

Me— What do you want me to do?

Roger:

Go—rest. Go in. You'll find good company—nothing to upset you. They'll make you drink Champagne.

Jeremy:

Not hard to get me to do that.

Roger:

Tell Mr. Edward that his father is back—but not to worry, I will wait for him here—and try to do all I can. I will sell myself to the devil if I know what! Tell him not to worry, and as for you, begin by getting drunk and go to bed.

Jeremy:

I will obey your orders exactly, don't fret.

(Exit Jeremy into the house)

Roger:

Come, Roger, pull yourself together my boy: courage! Here we have a violent father returning impromptu from a long trip; a son in the midst of an orgy; the house in disorder, full of cooks and caterers in preparation for an impending wedding—and all we have to do is prevent this from being discovered. Ah, here comes the old man. Let's stand aside a little and think of a way to prevent him from entering his own house.

(Enter Mr. Richly)

Richly:

Now after all my work and all the risks I've run— See: by Heaven's grace, my voyage has a happy ending. I return to my dear old home and I believe my son will be very happy to see me back and in good health.

Roger: (aside)

Not as happy as we would be to know you are well— but elsewhere.

Richly:

Children owe a good deal to fathers who work tirelessly to leave them well off.

Roger: (aside)

Yes, but not to those who return so inopportunely.

Richly:

I don't wish to delay anymore entering home and giving my son the pleasure of knowing I'm safely returned. I believe the poor boy will die of joy to see me.

Roger: (aside)

It wouldn't surprise me if he's already half dead just knowing you're here. But it's necessary to meet him.

(Aloud)

What do I see? Just Heaven—am I awake—is it a ghost?

Richly:

I believe if I am not deceived, that it's Roger.

Roger:

Indeed, it is Mr. Richly himself—or else the devil in his shape. Seriously speaking, is it you, my dear master?

Richly:

Yes, it's me, Roger. How've you been?

Roger:

As you see, sir, very much at your service like a faithful servant, bright-eyed and bushy-tailed—and always ready to obey you.

Richly:

That's good news. Let's go in.

Roger:

We weren't expecting you and I assure you, you have fallen on us from the clouds, as it were.

Richly:

No, I came by carriage from Portsmouth, where my ship happily arrived several days ago. But now—

Roger:

How well you look! What a face! How stout! The air in Spain must do wonders for men of your age. You ought to stay there, sir—for your health—

(Low)

—and our safety.

Richly:

And how is my son? Has he taken good care of the business? Is it profitable under his management?

Roger:

Oh, as to that, why I tell you, he has done so well—you wouldn't believe how he's into money. Your business is in a state that would astonish you—my word on it.

Richly:

You really make me happy, Roger, to give me such fine news. He's stored up a big pile of money, eh?

Roger:

Not at all, sir.

Richly:

Not at all? How's that!

Roger:

No, I tell you this boy is the best manager you could wish. He follows your footsteps. He drives your money like a race horse. If he can make a buck, he will work day and night.

Richly:

That comes from setting kids a good example. I'm dying with impatience to hug him. Come along, Roger.

Roger:

He's not inside, sir, and if you are in a hurry to see him, I suggest—

(Enter Mr. Andre)

Andre:

Good day, Roger—

Roger:

Your servant, Mr. Andre, your servant.

(Low)

Here's a villainous loan shark who picks a fine time to come demand his money.

Andre:

You know, Mr. Roger, I've been here every day lately without finding your master. If he cannot pay me today, tomorrow I will swear out a warrant against him and you know it very well.

Roger: (aside)

This will ruin us.

Richly:

What's this all about?

Roger:

I will explain everything to you when we are alone. Nothing to be concerned about!

Andre:

A mere business of one hundred pounds owed to me for

which I have a receipt and a judgment which I intend to put into execution.

Richly:

What's he talking about, Roger?

Roger:

He's a fiend who will do just what he says.

Richly:

Edward owes you—?

Andre:

Yes, indeed, Mr. Edward Richly, a child whose father is off somewhere, and who will be pleasantly surprised on his return when he learns of the life his son has led in his absence.

Roger:

This doesn't look too good.

Andre:

The son is a gambler, a spendthrift, and a wencher, while they say the father is a villain, a miser, and a tightass.

Richly:

What do you intend to say to this miser and tightass?

Andre:

I don't want to talk to you, I want to speak to the father of Mr. Edward Richly, who is in two words an imbecile and a fool.

Richly:

Roger—

Roger:

He's telling you the truth, sir. Mr. Edward does owe him—

Richly:

And you told me of his exemplary conduct.

Roger:

Yes, sir. It's a result of his careful management that he owes this money.

Richly:

What—borrow money from a loan shark?

(To Mr. Andre)

I see by looking at you, sir, that you're in the right line.

Andre:

Yes, sir, and I believe that you are also in the same profession.

Roger: (aside)

How easily honest men recognize each other.

Richly:

You dare to say this is the result of his superior management!

Roger:

Peace! Don't say a word. When you know the bottom of this thing, you will be enchanted. He has bought a house—a mansion for ten thousand pounds—

Richly:

A house for ten thousand?

Roger:

And easily worth fifteen. He didn't have enough cash, so in order not to lose the bargain, he borrowed money from this honest swindler you see here. You are not so angry as you were, I bet.

Richly:

On the contrary, I'm overjoyed. Oh, sir, this Mr. Edward who owes you the money is my son.

Roger:

And this gentleman is the father—got it?

Andre:

I'm overjoyed as well.

Richly:

Don't worry about your money. I approve what my son has done. Come back tomorrow and you will have your money—in cash.

Andre:

I'm your servant, sir.

(Exit Mr. Andre, delighted)

Richly:

Now tell me in what part of town is the house located?

Roger:

In what part of town?

Richly:

Yes, there are several neighborhoods. This one here, for example.

Roger:

Well, indeed, it's also located in this quarter.

Richly:

Good—so much the better. Where exactly?

Roger:

Hold on— (pointing) Do you see that house with an arbor where the windows have been repainted?

Richly:

Yes, well—?

Roger:

That's not it. But a little farther off. The one with the big gatehouse which is right next to the other one. Well, it's a little behind that on the next street. Catty-cornered to it.

Richly:

I don't see that one from here.

Roger:

I can't help that.

Richly:

Isn't that the home of Mrs. Prim?

Roger:

Right. Mrs. Prim. Couldn't remember her name. Good buy, isn't it?

Richly:

Absolutely. But why did the stupid woman sell off her inheritance?

Roger:

One can't foresee everything that will happen in life, as the philosophers say. She's been very unfortunate—she's gone plum crazy.

Richly:

Gone crazy?

Roger:

Raving. Her family tried to stop her. And her son who is a rake gave his house for a fraction of the money hers was worth.

(Low)

I'm getting in deeper and deeper.

Richly:

But she doesn't have any son that I know of.

Roger:

She doesn't have a son?

Richly:

No. I'm sure of it.

Roger:

Must have been her daughter then.

Richly:

I'm irritated by this mischance. But I've amused myself long enough. Open the door for me, will you?

Roger: (low)

Ouf! Now we've reached the crisis.

Richly:

What's the matter? Has something happened to my son?

Roger:

No, sir.

Richly:

Has someone stolen something in my absence?

Roger:

Not at all.

(Low)

What will I tell him?

Richly:

Explain everything. Speak.

Roger:

I can hardly keep from crying. Don't go in, sir. Your house—this dear house—which you love—has for the last six months—

Richly:

Well—my house—for the last six months—

Roger:

The devil is haunting the place, sir. He made us take up residence elsewhere.

Richly:

The devil is in my house?

Roger:

Yes, sir. Haunts the place. In fact, that's what has forced your son to buy another house. We couldn't live there anymore.

Richly:

You're kidding me. It isn't possible.

Roger:

There's no sort of malicious trick they haven't put on me. Sometimes they mock me when I'm unable to move my feet. Sometimes they shave my beard with a red hot razor—and without fail every night they affront me with the stench of sulfur.

Richly:

And now I say again, you're putting me on.

Roger:

Not at all, sir. What hasn't happened to me? We've brought the best exorcists in London. There's no way to force them out; this spirit is furiously tenacious—he's the one that possesses women when they have the devil in them.

Richly:

A horrible thought has occurred to me. Tell me, I beg you, have they been in the wine cellar?

Roger:

Alas, sir, they forage everywhere.

Richly:

I am lost. I buried fifty thousand pounds in that wine cellar.

Roger:

Fifty thousand pounds! Sir, there are fifty thousand pounds in your house?

Richly:

In the wine cellar.

Roger:

In the wine cellar. That's exactly where they hold their Sabbath.— Oh, if only we had known this. And where in the wine cellar, if you please?

Richly:

To the left as you enter. Under a big block of stone near the door.

Roger:

Fifty thousand pounds under a big block of stone! You should have told us—we could have saved you from this unlucky pass. It's on the left as you go in, you say.

Richly:

Yes. The place is easy to find.

Roger:

I'll easily find it. But you know, sir, that it's worth your life— you're risking your neck to go in there? And the whole sum is in gold?

Richly:

All in pure gold.

Roger: (aside)

Good. Easier to carry.

(Aloud)

Oh, as to that, sir, since we know the cause of the evil, it won't be hard to find a remedy. I believe we'll—manage. Leave it to me.

Richly:

I have trouble believing all you tell me. You tell me so many stories about these matters that I don't know what to believe. I'll trust you for now, but I'll find out what's what. What reversals one sees in life! One can't make a little money without men or the devil trying to get it away from you. The devil is not going to have it!

(Exit Richly)

(Enter Lucy)

Lucy:

Ah, my poor Roger. Is it true that Mr. Edward's father has returned?

Roger:

Only too true, but to console us, I have found a treasure.

Lucy:

A treasure?

Roger:

In the wine cellar, as you enter—to the left under a large black stone—a sack which contains fifty thousand pounds.

Lucy:

Fifty thousand pounds.

Roger:

Yes, child, and I tell you that will be plenty—run, find the sack, the sack—hurry!

Lucy:

But—

Roger:

The devil take you with your buts. Mr. Richly will return. Save yourself—hide, quickly. To the treasure.

To the treasure.

(Exit Lucy)

We are about to have a nice explanation. Now to navigate your ship and bring it into port.

(Reenter Richly)

Richly:

You see, I wasn't long. I found my porters near here and I've told them to wait because it seems a good idea to store my goods in the house my son has bought.

Roger:

A new fix!

Richly:

I don't recognize the place too well, so you can take me there yourself.

Roger:

I want to, sir, but—

Richly:

But what! The Devil isn't master there, too, is he?

Roger:

Mrs. Prim is still living there.

Richly:

Still living there?

Roger:

Yes, indeed. It's agreed that she will stay out her term, and—as her mind is weak—she gets in a furious state whenever anyone talks to her about vacating. She's really crazy, you see.

Richly:

I'll talk to her in a way that will calm her down.

Roger:

You!

(Aside)

All is lost.

Richly:

You're making me very impatient. I absolutely want to speak to her, I tell you.

Roger:

Well, in that case—talk to her—because happily, here she comes. But remember she's a basket case.

Mrs. Prim: (entering)

Well, here's Mr. Richly returned, it seems.

Roger: (low to Mrs. Prim)

Yes, Madam, indeed it is he—but he's lost his wits. His ship was wrecked and he drank salt water. It turned his head.

Mrs. Prim:

What a shame—the poor man!

Roger:

If he happens by chance to accost you, he may say something odd. Don't pay any attention. We're going to have him locked up.

(To Richly)

If you speak to her, have a little patience with her weakness. Think of her as a clock that's a bit cuckoo.

Richly:

Leave her to me.

Mrs. Prim:

There's something strange and distracted about his manner.

Richly:

How her looks have changed. She has haggard eyes.

Mrs. Prim:

Well—it's Mr. Richly. You've come back to England, eh?

Richly:

Ready to render you my devoirs.

Mrs. Prim:

I'm very distressed about the misfortune you've suffered.

Richly:

I have to be patient. They say devils are occupying my house. But it will be all right after we kick them out. They'll be worn out staying there.

Mrs. Prim: (aside)

Devils in his house! I'd better not contradict him, it might make him worse.

Richly:

I'd like, madam, to store some packages that I brought back with me in your house.

Mrs. Prim: (aside)

He doesn't realize that his ship was wrecked. What a pity.

(Aloud)

I am at your service and my house is more yours than mine.

Richly:

Oh, madam, I have no intention of abusing you of the condition you are in.

(To Roger)

But really, Roger, this woman is not as crazy as you said she was.

Roger:

She has a few good moments—but it won't last.

Richly:

Tell me, Mrs. Prim, have you always been as wise and as reasonable as you are now?

Mrs. Prim:

I don't think anybody, Mr. Richly, has ever seen me otherwise.

Richly:

But if that's so, your family shouldn't have you locked up.

Mrs. Prim:

Locked up—me—have me locked up?

Richly: (aside)

She's totally unaware of her illness.

Mrs. Prim:

But if you are not ordinarily more crazy than at present, I think it's very wrong you should be put away.

Richly:

Me put away?

(Aside)

Now she's out of whack; there it is, there it is. Let's change the subject.

(Aloud)

Well, is it that you're irritated about their selling your house?

Mrs. Prim:

They sold my house?

Richly:

At least it's better that my son bought it at a bargain price.

Mrs. Prim:

My poor Mr. Richly. My house hasn't been sold, and it's not for sale.

Richly:

There! There! Don't upset yourself, I promise you you will always have your apartment—just as if you still owned it—and as if you were in good mental health.

Mrs. Prim:

What do you mean, as if I was still in good mental health! Go away, you're an old madman, an old madman who shouldn't be allowed out of Bedlam—of Bedlam, my friend.

Roger: (To Mrs. Prim)

Are you wise to fight with a wacko?

Richly:

Oh, if that's your attitude, you can get out. The house belongs to me, and I'll put my luggage there in spite of you. Just look at this crazy old woman.

Roger: (To Richly)

What are you getting in a rage for with a woman who has lost her mind?

Mrs. Prim:

Just try. I'll be waiting for you. Back to your padded cell, you lunatic! Hurry and lock him up, he's becoming dangerous, I'm warning you.

(Exit Mrs. Prim in a huff)

Roger: (aside)

I don't quite know how I am going to get out of this.

Squire: (entering from the house)

What's all this hullabaloo? Beating on an honest man's door and scandalizing the neighborhood?

Richly:

Roger, what's going on?

Roger:

The devils in your house are a little drunk. They frolic in the wine cellar.

Richly:

Some kind of swindle is afoot, I'm sure of it.

Squire:

They say the master of this house has just returned from a long sea voyage—would you be he by any chance?

Richly:

Yes, sir, I am he.

Squire:

I congratulate you, sir. That was a beautiful trip and a wonderful lesson for a young man. You must know, sir, that your son has been learning wonderful manners while you were gone. Really fine manners. The boy is very generous. Doesn't resemble you at all. You are a villain, sir.

Richly:

Sir, sir!

Roger:

These teasing devils are insolent.

Richly:

You are a rogue.

Squire:

We were very upset, very worried—full of concern over your return. In your absence your son was ready to kill himself from malaise. In truth, he disliked everything in life. He gave up all his vanities. Everything that could attach him to this earth: wealth, furniture, honors. This boy loves you so much it's unbelievable.

Roger:

He would have died of worry during your absence if it hadn't been for this honest gentleman.

Richly:

He! How is it you're in my house, sir, if you please?

Squire:

Don't you understand without my telling you? I've just drunk champagne in the best company. He's still feasting, which is the best way possible for him to comfort himself in your absence.

Richly:

This swindler will ruin me. I'm going in.

Roger:

Stop! I will not allow you to enter.

Richly:

I can't go in to my own house?

Squire:

No. The company is not ready to receive you.

Richly:

What do you mean?

Squire:

It wouldn't be proper for a son who knows how to live and who has been learning manners from me to receive his father in a house which has nothing in it but the four walls.

Richly:

What—four walls? My beautiful paintings which cost me three thousand pounds—are they gone?

Squire:

We got eighteen hundred for them. Not a bad sale.

Richly:

Not a bad sale. Masterpieces like that.

Squire:

Bah! The subject was lugubrious. The fall of Troy with a villainous wooden horse that had neither mouth nor tail. We made a friend out of the buyer.

Richly:

Ah, gallows bird.

Squire:

Weren't there a couple of other paintings that represented something?

Richly:

Oh, yes. They were originals by a master some think to be Leonardo—they represented the Rape of the Sabines.

Squire:

Right. We got rid of them, too—because of delicacy of conscience.

Richly:

Delicacy of conscience!

Squire:

A wise, virtuous, religious man like Mr. Richly—and to have immodest, nude, Sabine women about him—fie! Nudity is not for the young.

(Reenter Mrs. Prim)

Mrs. Prim:

Ah, truly, I have just been warned of some nice business, Mr. Richly. They say your son is marrying my niece.

Richly:

I don't know about your niece, but my son is a rogue, Mrs. Prim.

Roger:

Yes, a rake who has led me astray and who has caused—

Squire:

Let's not complain about each other or speak ill of those who are not present. One shouldn't condemn people without hearing them first. Pay attention, if you please, Mr. Richly. You've got to look on the bright side. If you are happy, the whole world will be happy. Besides, it's not your fault. And you can't do anything about it but kick up a fuss. If you are patient, no one will laugh at you.

Richly:

Go to the devil with your sophistries. But what do I see. They're running off with my fifty thousand pounds.

Mrs. Prim:

It's that bitch of a Lucy and my niece.

Richly:

And my swindler son.

(Enter Edward and the others)

Edward:

Daddy, it's no longer necessary to abuse your credulity. All this has been due to the zeal of Roger to keep you out of the house while I married Belinda. I ask you to pardon my past behavior. Bless this marriage, I beg you.

(Low)

Then you can have your fifty thousand back, and I promise to be better in the future.

Richly:

Ah, gallows bird, do you mock me?

Roger:

It's true, sir.

Mrs. Prim:

Belinda is my niece—and if your son has married her, I'll give her a dowry which will satisfy you.

Richly:

Can you do that? Aren't you under restraint?

Roger:

That was only my trick.

Richly:

What? The house—?

Roger:

Part of the same thing.

Richly:

What a misfortune! But if you will give me my money back, I've got enough sense of humor to give my consent, if you want it. It's the only way to prevent worse from happening.

Squire:

Well, said. That pleases me. Shake, Mr. Richly—you're a brave man. I want to drink with you. Let's go back in and have more to drink and eat. You know, it was a lucky thing you came just in time for the wedding.

CURTAIN

THE RIDICULOUS MERCHANT: A COMIC OPERA

CAST OF CHARACTERS

THE MARQUIS

POLICHINELLE, his valet

JANBROCHE, a draper

MISS JANBROCHE, his daughter

PIERROT, Janbroche's valet

THE COLLEAGUE

THE PLAY

JANBROCHE:

(to Colleague) Sir, I am your servant. Could you do me a pleasure?

COLLEAGUE:

What pleasure do you want from me?

JANBROCHE:

I really want to beg you to take care of my shop, and especially my daughter.

COLLEAGUE:

Sir, for such a difficulty, I don't care; but you have your servant Pierrot who will do your business.

JANBROCHE:

Indeed, you are not very obliging. I am going to call my servant. Pierrot, hola, Pierrot!

(The Colleague leaves, Pierrot enters.)

PIERROT:

Sir, what, what's to be done for your service?

JANBROCHE:

You must stand in for me, and be the steward of my house.

PIERROT:

My word, sir, I cannot serve as the column of your building.

JANBROCHE:

It's to take care of my shop and to have special care of my daughter.

PIERROT:

My word, sir, I would really like to take care of your shop, but not your daughter, because she's merchandise like water of the Queen of Hungary: as soon as you allow, it goes flat—the savor goes, a daughter is the same. So, sir, you can keep her yourself.

JANBROCHE:

Go, go, scoundrel that you are, go tell my daughter to

come speak to me.

PIERROT:

Sir, I am going instantly.

(Exit Pierrot, enter Miss Janbroche.)

MISS JANBROCHE:

What do you want, my dear father?

JANBROCHE:

Daughter, come close when I speak to you; I am going to leave to go purchase some drapes that I need, and I want nothing to be sold in my shop during my absence.

MISS JANBROCHE:

That would seem completely ridiculous.

JANBROCHE:

It's because of that that I am called, The Ridiculous Merchant.

MISS JANBROCHE:

But, my dear father, in what manner do you want me to dismiss the merchants?

JANBROCHE:

Daughter, when some merchant comes to you to ask for drapes, and says to you: "Miss, don't you have a fine Holland drape to sell me?" He must be replied to: "Truly, not at all, sir." In that way you will keep your honor and your reputation.

MISS JANBROCHE:

That suffices, my dear father, I won't fail to do it.

JANBROCHE:

Goodbye, my little girl.

MISS JANBROCHE:

Goodbye, my dear papa.

(Janbroche leaves, as does his daughter. After a short pause The Marquis and Polichinelle enter.)

MARQUIS:

Tell me, rogue, how long have I been looking for you and where have you been?

POLICHINELLE:

My word, sir, I was making some verse in the water-closet.

MARQUIS:

What, impertinent. Is that a place to make verse?

POLICHINELLE:

Why, sir, everybody does it where he can. What do you want with me?

MARQUIS:

You must go right away on my behalf to the home of Mr. Janbroche, my customary supplier, to find me a complete outfit for a gentleman.

POLICHINELLE:

But, sir, without being too curious, for what purpose?

MARQUIS:

It's because I'm on the point of getting married.

POLICHINELLE:

Why, sir, why don't you put yourself in lace? That's better suited than stitching point.

MARQUIS:

Animal that you are, that's not it; I mean to take a wife.

POLICHINELLE:

Ah! Sir, I hear you: is it because you know I need a wife, you are taking one for yourself and me as well?

MARQUIS:

Impertinent, that you are: know that I am taking a wife; that's not for an impertinent like you, and she's for me.

POLICHINELLE:

Well, sir, if in any case she gets lost, you can search for her all alone.

MARQUIS:

Yeah, yeah, not so much verbiage, do my errand as quickly as possible.

POLICHINELLE:

But, sir, where's he live?

MARQUIS:

Heavens, there's the door. March.

POLICHINELLE:

That's fine, sir, I'm going there. (to Colleague) Go, go, Colleague. I'm really going to shoe a mule.

COLLEAGUE:

But why do you want to shoe a mule? They didn't give you the money.

POLICHINELLE:

You are right again, I'm going to call him. (running after the Marquis) Sir, sir, you didn't give me any money.

MARQUIS:

Go on, go on, he's my customary merchant, I only pay him annually.

POLICHINELLE:

Right. Now that's not bad for us; I was counting on shoeing a mule, and I won't shoe just one. (raps on Janbroche's door)

(Exit the Marquis.)

POLICHINELLE:

Mr. Janbroche, I am your servant.

COLLEAGUE:

Impertinent that you are, don't you see that it's Miss, his daughter?

POLICHINELLE:

Well I—I prefer to kiss the daughter to the father. Miss, have you drapes from Holland?

MISS JANBROCHE:

Truly, not at all, sir.

(Polichinelle continues to ask Miss Janbroche for several sorts of drapes)

Truly, not at all, sir.

(A footnote says: we thought we were duty bound to suppress some lines of dialogue because of their triviality.)

(Janbroche returns from his trip and asks the Colleague what has happened during his absence.)

COLLEAGUE:

My, word, sir, I don't know a thing, and moreover, you can call your servant Pierrot.

JANBROCHE:

Pierrot!

PIERROT:

(entering) Sir, since I saw you last there's been a lot of news.

JANBROCHE:

What news?

PIERROT:

The males are sleeping with the females.

JANBROCHE:

Beast that you are, that's been happening all the time and will continue to happen.

PIERROT:

Well, sir, since it has to be, I am telling you, there's a big fat boy sleeping with your daughter.

JANBROCHE:

(wanting to strike Pierrot) What! A boy sleeping with my daughter! Now I'm going to lose honor and reputation.

PIERROT:

Why, sir—why, sir—let youth divert itself.

(Janbroche enters the house and chases Polichinelle, who appears in his underwear.)

POLICHINELLE:

(coming out of the house) But, sir, give me back my breeches.

JANBROCHE:

(pushing Polichinelle and striking him with a stick) Wait, here's your breeches.

MARQUIS:

(entering with Colleague) Sir, tell me a little, haven't you seen my rogue of a servant?

POLICHINELLE:

Sir, here I am.

(The Marquis, seeing Polichinelle in his underwear, draws his sword with the intent of running him through.)

POLICHINELLE:

(on his knees) Ah! Sir, if you're going to smash the mustard pot, it's going to squirt in your eyes.

MARQUIS:

Wretch, whose outfit are you wearing?

POLICHINELLE:

While I was going to bathe, sir, some little thieves stole my breeches.

MARQUIS:

Scoundrel, if you don't tell me the truth, I am going to beat you unmercifully with blows from a stick, instantly.

POLICHINELLE:

Sir, wait, don't put yourself in a rage. I am going to tell you the truth; as the daughter of Mr. Janbroche was afraid, she begged me to go to bed with her, and me, very obliging as I am, I couldn't refuse her.

MARQUIS:

Go, go, you are a wretch; you've got to marry her.

POLICHINELLE:

Right, right, so much the better, now here's my business.

(They return Polichinelle's clothes, and male and

female dancers celebrate the wedding.)

CURTAIN

ABOUT THE TRANSLATOR

Frank J. Morlock has written and translated many plays since retiring from the legal profession in 1992. His translations have also appeared on Project Gutenberg, the Alexandre Dumas Père web page, Literature in the Age of Napoléon, Infinite Artistries.com, and Munsey's (formerly Blackmask). In 2006 he received an award from the North American Jules Verne Society for his translations of Verne's plays. He lives and works in México.

www.ingramcontent.com/pod-product-compliance
Lightning Source LLC
LaVergne TN
LVHW041620070426
835507LV00008B/352